The Officia
Buying Final Expense
Life Insurance

David M. Duford

This publication is designed to provide accurate and authoritative information in regard to the subject matter covered. It is sold with the understanding that the publisher and author are not engaged in rendering legal, accounting, insurance, or other professional services. If legal advice or other expert assistance is required, the services of a competent professional should be south.

ISBN:1983943363
ISBN-13:978-1983943362

DEDICATION

This book is dedicated to the 1500+ final expense life insurance clients that trusted me with their insurance concerns. Thanks for helping me become a success!

The Official Guide To Buying Final Expense Life Insurance

CONTENTS

1 THE DEFINITIVE GUIDE TO BUYING BURIAL INSURANCE

As a specialist in the burial insurance business, people often ask, "What is the BEST kind of burial life insurance?"

That's a great question. And more likely than not, you see numerous options for burial insurance for seniors every single day. For example, there are endless advertisements on TV from Colonial Penn, MetLife, Mutual of Omaha, and Physicians Mutual. And don't forget all the junk mail that you receive daily from a variety of burial insurance companies.

Sometimes, when there are too many options, it's downright confusing, and can cause people who really need a burial insurance policy to not do anything at all.

In the following article, I will go into detail about different options for burial life insurance coverage. Naturally, the goal is to give you as much information possible on how different final expense burial insurance policies work, as well as how to better examine what your best options are for burial life insurance coverage.

Term Life Burial Insurance

The first final expense burial insurance for seniors option I'll cover is what's known as term life insurance. Perhaps you've received mailers from AARP or Globe Life Insurance. Upon reading the letters they send, many times you'll discover these companies only offer coverage up to and no further than a certain age in the future. This is what we call "terminating," or term, insurance. The key word is TERMINATING.

What's the problem with term life insurance?

First of all, term life insurance for final expenses do not appropriately match the primary reason people buy burial insurance for seniors. And here's the truth – the primary reason behind buying a burial insurance policy is to **guarantee a death benefit, no matter at what age you pass away**.

Why do you need your burial insurance death benefit guaranteed? Because death is uncertain! You WILL die, guaranteed!

Therefore, getting a term life insurance policy for burial insurance begs the question,

"Why take the risk of not having coverage when you need it?"

How A Term Life Insurance Policy For A Senior Went From $50 To $350 A Month!

Several years back as a new burial insurance agent, I met a very nice 82-year-old lady. She worked in the cleaners her entire life and was still working 20 hours a week dry cleaning. Her health was great and all was well.

Regarding her burial insurance policy, she had a plan from a very well-known company. Her plan was a term insurance plan. And while this plan didn't cancel until she reached 90, the term insurance premium increased annually for the past 12 years.

What started off around $50 a month for her term insurance **was now $350 a month**. Nevertheless, she could afford it since she worked part-time and had drew Social Security.

How Burial Life Insurance Can Become Unaffordable Overnight

Unfortunately, her health took a change for the worse. The doctors recommended open heart surgery to fix a blockage. And since she was 82, the doctor ordered her into retirement.

Since she lost her income from her part-time job, she was now in a tough position. Bills had to be paid, and there was no room to afford a $350 term insurance premium. And to add insult to injury, she could get to replace her term insurance policy with immediate coverage with another burial insurance policy option. Due to her recent open-heart surgery experience, her only option was a 2-year waiting period burial insurance policy (which will discuss in more detail shortly).

This sad story happens daily. People do a good job of having burial insurance policy in place. However, they don't understand how it works. And usually it's because the final expense burial insurance agent didn't explain it. Even worse, the agent may have purposely hidden the facts from them.

Now well into retirement, this lady doesn't have either the means to pay for expensive term life insurance, or the health to qualify for something better. Whatever you do, don't be this person.

Permanent Burial Insurance Policy Options

Regarding burial insurance for seniors, the opposite of a term insurance policy is a permanent policy. A permanent burial insurance policy is permanent as long as you pay the premium. For your whole life, regardless of how long you live, you receive guaranteed coverage to provide a specific death benefit payable to the beneficiary of your choice.

Like myself, burial agents commonly recommend permanent burial insurance for seniors to those looking for final expense coverage. Why? *Because the design of the policy matches the reality of the problem.*

Guarantees In Your Burial Insurance Policy

As mentioned earlier, a burial insurance policy that does NOT cover you past a certain age doesn't do you any good. With a permanent burial insurance policy, as long as you pay your premium, you have coverage. And you'll never be in a situation where you outlive it! When you do pass away, assuming the premiums are current, the policy pays the death benefit as directed in the policy.

Within the category of permanent coverage, there are several different options. Your goal is to find a policy you or your loved one (if you're a spouse or child shopping for burial insurance on a parent) can qualify for.

What follows is a breakdown of the different options for permanent coverage.

Guaranteed Acceptance Burial Insurance Policy

First of all, you have guaranteed acceptance whole life insurance.
Guaranteed acceptance insurance means that **the policy will be issued under any circumstance, regardless of health**. Beyond age limits, the company cannot decline you. Simply put, if you have a pulse and can sign your name, you're approved. This is a great policy option for people who are otherwise uninsurable, like those with Alzheimer's, current cancer (those who have been cancer-free for over a year have better options), and kidney dialysis.

As you can imagine, there are drawbacks. Let me explain. Generally speaking, a guaranteed issue burial insurance policy provides first-day 100% full coverage for accidental death only. Death caused by natural reasons are **not** fully covered for minimum of the first 2 years.

Here's the truth. Most seniors die from natural reasons, and not accidental death. Therefore, if guaranteed acceptance burial insurance for seniors is your only option, you won't have natural death coverage until 2 years after the effective date of the policy.

Why Would One Get A Guaranteed Issue Burial Life Insurance Policy?

The main reason to buy a guaranteed issue policy is because **one has tried other options first**. They've tried to get full coverage elsewhere and have simply not qualified for it. Therefore, a guaranteed acceptance life insurance policy is the last choice you should pursue.

The big problem with no questions asked life insurance is this: it is commonly offered to the public *as the first choice for burial insurance*! Shockingly, the most common options available for burial insurance for guaranteed acceptance insurance.

You should highly consider talking with a burial life insurance agent that may have the option to provide you full first-day or even partial first-day coverage.

Why? Because death is uncertain. And while many of us assume we'll live a long time, we all know deep down that we'll never know our final day. Our time is limited. We don't know when it'll be, and we have to be prepared regardless, which brings us to the next option: full coverage burial insurance for seniors.

Burial Insurance With Whole Life

The ideal scenario is to qualify for a day-one, full-coverage burial insurance whole life policy. Luckily, this is not a very difficult process.

However, not all burial insurance whole life options are equal. Let's break it down further and explain the difference between working with a **broker** versus a **captive agent**.

Captive Agents

If you are beholden to one insurance company or agency, then you are a "captive" agent. In the world of burial insurance, the captive agent typically represents only one company. Since captive agents' options are limited to one company, they must only offer one coverage option to you, the client.

And while that may sound fine, the problem is this: one option is usually not a good option for the vast majority of people!

If working with a captive agent is not in your best interest, what is?

Independent Agents

You want to work with someone who offers more than one choice for burial life insurance. Why? Because with a captive agent, you lose, either on quality of coverage or pricing.

Let's compare buying burial insurance to buying groceries. When it's time to shop, would you go to a store that only sells **one** type of meat, **one** type of bread, and **one** type of vegetable? Or would prefer a store with a variety of options for food at better prices?

It's the same with burial insurance. To clarify, if your agent only offers one type of product, you'll most likely end up paying more for less coverage. Whereas if you worked with an independent agent, you may have had a much higher chance for the best combination of pricing and value for your burial insurance.

How To Get Low-price, High-quality Burial Insurance

So, what is the solution? The best option is to work with an independent agent. An independent agent is somebody who offers the best burial insurance policies available. And "best" defined as a variety of competitively priced products that have flexible underwriting. An independent agent is somebody who doesn't just work with one insurance company. They work with many burial insurance companies. And they take the client's needs and goals into consideration when helping them select a burial insurance policy.

Many times, a person working with an independent burial life insurance agent will get more coverage and save hundreds of dollars year! Also, the burial insurance policy will often cover issues that the captive agent could not cover.

For example, common issues that can be covered with an independent burial insurance agent include conditions such as COPD, heart history issues, diabetes, cancer, kidney and liver problems, neurological problems, and mental health problems. Unfortunately, in many cases, captive agents can only offer you high-priced guaranteed acceptance policies. However, an independent agent may be able to offer you full first-day coverage policies!

Ultimately, if you think burial insurance whole life is right for you, find an independent agent who shops the major companies for you to find you the best price and the best coverage.

Other Burial Insurance For Seniors Options

There are other options for burial insurance for seniors, beyond term life and whole life options. Read below for more information on other types of burial life insurance options, chiefly designed for very healthy applicants, and those who have more means to pay higher premiums.

Pre-need Burial Insurance Policy

The first option is pre-need insurance coverage.

Pre-need insurance is a burial insurance policy purchased through a funeral home. Pre-need policies are a bit different than burial insurance policies. First, pre-need plans are designed to lock in your rates for all the items associated with your funeral. Items like your casket, cremation expense, the service itself, etc. are locked in and guaranteed.

The policy also is a paid-up policy. This means you pay premiums over 5 to 10 years before paying it off completely. If death occurs prior to you paying the policy off, in most circumstances the policy pays the death benefit to cover the funeral expense of death. With pre-need burial life insurance policies, they act as an insurance policy, but also has the added advantage of combating the inflationary costs of funerals.

The pros a pre-need funeral policy is that your premiums will eventually end, and you'll pay the funeral off completely. Many people opt for a 3- to 5-year payoff plan. However, the less financially able choose the 7- to 10-year payoff plans.

Pre-need Life Insurance Can Be Very Expensive!

The cons of pre-need plans are that they are generally 2-3 times as expensive. And while many people like pre-need policies, they cannot comfortably afford it.

To make matters worse, when the premiums paid into a pre-need policy are added up, **the total exceeds the actual cost of the funeral**.

I've seen many pre-need policies where premiums paid in **are more than DOUBLE** than the cost of the funeral. Also, I've seen instances where the total cost of the funeral was $8000-$10,000 whereas the actual premiums paid in was $15,000-$20,000!

In my mind, these plans are problematic for most. Certainly, fending off inflation is great. But one must believe it's worth paying nearly double the current price for a funeral to do so. I think not!

Pricing for funerals has remained pretty stable since I've been in the business back in 2011. And as long as that's the reality, I don't see pre-need insurance as an option, unless you pay it up in under 5 years or less. At those levels, the premiums paid in are more sensible.

The biggest advantage to pre-need insurance is paying it up. Luckily, you have access to the same paid-up options with a burial life insurance plan. And in many cases, the premium for a paid-up burial insurance policy is much lower. Also, the underwriting regarding burial insurance for seniors is more flexible than pre-need insurance plans. So consider working with an independent burial life insurance agent if you like the paid-up concept.

Guaranteed Universal Life For Burial Insurance

Are you in good health and interested in burial insurance policy sizes in excess of $25,000 in coverage? Consider a guaranteed universal life insurance policy.

The idea behind a guaranteed universal life insurance policy is similar to a burial insurance whole life plan. However, the biggest difference is minimal access to cash value. And the reason for this is that a guaranteed universal life plan maximizes the amount of death benefit payable. In return, you see limited cash value access.

I only recommend guaranteed universal life insurance if someone is looking for a substantial amount of coverage. The applicant also needs to be in very good health. Underwriting is a bit tighter, and the client needs to clearly understand the lack of long-term cash value access.

Nevertheless, guaranteed universal life insurance plans are great for people who want a large death benefit.

Summary On Burial Insurance Options

Now you must ask, what is the best course of action to pursue?

Start with an analysis of your needs. For example, what do you want to accomplish with your burial insurance policy?

Maybe you want only enough coverage to pay for your burial. Or, maybe you don't want to leave a legacy to a child or grandchild. Furthermore, you may want to leave a nice death benefit to replace your family's income. Establish what your personal goals are, then select a burial policy above that best fits you.

For most people I work with, a burial insurance whole life product is the best coverage option. Why? Burial insurance whole life combines easier underwriting, competitive pricing, and permanent coverage without future rate increases.

Ideally, work with an independent agent to give yourself the best shot for first-day full coverage. If you end up only qualifying for guaranteed acceptance life insurance, make sure your agent shops other companies. But if they do and all you can get is a guaranteed issue burial life insurance plan, then highly consider keeping it.

2 EXPERT ADVICE FOR CONSUMERS ON FINAL EXPENSE WHOLE LIFE INSURANCE

What Is Final Expense Whole Life Insurance?

Final expense whole life insurance is defined as life insurance coverage to cover costs related to funerals, burials, and cremation expenses. Final expenses include funeral items such as the casket, plot, and urn. Additional expenses include the service, delivery fees, flowers, and so forth.

Not sure if you have enough money to cover the final expense above? If so, then final expense whole life insurance is worth considering.

Hundreds of thousands of people have a final expense whole life insurance plan to cover these expenses. Why? Because they're not sure they have the ability to pay on-demand, out-of-pocket. The lack of ready-to-use savings for events such as death is a big reason why people buy in the first place.

Generally, final expense whole life insurance plans offer smaller death benefits. Most don't buy a million-dollar final expense plan. And while it can be done, people more commonly purchase a plan that's just enough to cover for a burial. And usually a policy between $10,000 to $25,000 is common.

Final expense whole life insurance policies can go small than $10,000. I've helped people out with $2,000 or $3,000 plans, since all that's necessary is simple cremation.

Most final expense whole life insurance plans are what we call simplified issue. There are no examinations or physicals. You simply complete an application, and that's that! However, there are times when you must complete a phone interview to assess your health prior to approval.

With final expense whole life insurance plans, you either qualify or you don't. Phone interviews, which typically last for only 10 minutes, tell us instantly whether you're approved. You get an instant "yes or no" decision, which is what we really want in this business.

Why Get A Final Expense Whole Life Insurance Program?

Why buy final expense whole life insurance? Let's cover 4 primary reasons why people like you purchase a burial insurance plan.

1. Funeral Costs

The top reason to purchase final expense whole life insurance is to eliminate the fear of not having sufficient money to pay for funeral expenses. This accounts for 80 to 90% of the reasons why people purchase a final expense plan.

Let me put it plainly. Are you worried that when you die, your spouse or kids won't have enough money on-hand to pay your burial? If so, a final expense whole life insurance plan is worth considering.

Many people who purchase a final expense whole life insurance plan are on a fixed income. They have reached retirement. And guess what? They're not rich!

And while they may have a pension, it's not substantial. And what they have in savings isn't great, either.

Considering the above, people who buy final expense whole life insurance understand that death is unpredictable. It's something that often happens suddenly. And there just isn't enough time to save up enough money to pay for funeral expenses.

2. Income Replacement

A second reason to buy whole life final expense insurance is the fear of a spouse living with less. Simply put, you're worried your spouse's income will reduce his or her lifestyle.

As an insurance agent that sell final expense whole life insurance, I help people with these concerns regularly. Picture your loved ones having less money to live on. Would it dramatically alter her lifestyle?

Maybe she doesn't get to do the normal things she's accustomed to. Maybe she's forced to change health insurance. Or maybe she can't get the medications she needs because the money isn't just there.

If you're concerned that your death may dramatically affect your survivors living, then a final expense plan is a perfect solution.

Case in point, I have a gentleman who was 85 when he purchased $125,000 in coverage. While this was an unusually large sum, he wanted to leave money behind to supplement his income for his wife.

He passed away six months later. And all the policies paid! It made a dramatic difference in his wife's life because of how important he felt owning final expense whole life insurance was.

3. Non-funeral Related Costs

The third reason people own final expense whole life insurance is to relieve the financial burden from the "what-ifs" from spouse and family.

When it comes to non-funeral related final expenses, things happen. You may have savings today. But something may happen where the savings must be used.

Here's a perfect example. I met a retired police officer in Alabama a few years back. He had a great pension and a lot of money saved up. His wife was retired as a teacher.

Unfortunately, his daughter got into the wrong crowd, and became addicted to drugs. And if you know anything about addiction, it is a costly endeavor to deal with.

His daughter was in her 20s when this happened, right at the peak of his retirement from the police force. He drained all his savings to bail her out of jail and pay for her rehab several times.

This unforeseen tragedy altered his lifestyle for the worse. And if you had asked him when his daughter was born if this was going to happen, he would have never expected it.

And that's the reason he has final expense whole life insurance. Because he wanted to have a plan set aside to cover those expenses that may arise.

People buy these plans to play it safe. And that's a legitimate reason to own a final expense whole life insurance policy. Why? Because no one knows what's going to happen day-to-day. Things happen unexpectedly, and requirements for money usually never go away. They intensify and increase as you get older.

4. Leaving A Legacy

The last reason to own a final expense whole life insurance plan is to leave a legacy.

Like I mentioned about my mom earlier, she had a new roof put on with the $7,000 policy my grandfather left. These gifts of life insurance always help loved ones at the perfect time.

So if you're compassionate, loving, and you feel a tug on your heart to do this, a final expense whole life policy is perfect as a solution to make this work.

"Fun" Facts Of Final Expenses

Let's talk about some funeral expense "fun" facts. I put "fun" in quotes because there's no fun in funeral! Well, I guess there is fun in funeral but not the kind of fun I want!

Again, one of the main reasons people buy final expense whole life insurance is to fund their funeral so their family doesn't.

1. Average National Cost Of Burial Expenses

In 2014, the National Funeral Directors Association_estimated the average burial funeral in 2014 cost approximately $8,500. And based off my real-world experience, I would say that is an accurate average.

In the survey, the NFDA broke down all the component costs of a burial and a cremation (we'll get to cremation in a minute). They looked at the transportation cost, the flowers, the casket, and everything associated with a funeral.

2. Cremation Expenses

Nationally, the NFDA found in 2014 the average cremation cost is $6,100. Personally, I feel this number is rather inflated.

Here's why. The NFDA is accounting for a full funeral service as well as the cremation expense. Probably like you, I've seen plenty of cremations in the $3,000 range or less.

So, if you're a bit surprised at this number, you're probably right to be suspicious!

I wonder how the NFDA did their math. I've never seen but maybe one or two cremations that have been this high. Most are much less expensive. Nevertheless, understand that NFDA says this is the national average.

Many people nowadays end up getting a direct cremation. Perhaps there is only a small service at a church. For my grandfather, we had his wake at the Rotary Club at no cost. If you go all out and do the service, then you're looking at a price that's high.

Here's the kicker. You all have been around long enough to know prices go up as you get older. From 2004 to 2014, a span of 10 years, funeral costs rose 28.6%!

The NFDA shows the average funeral experienced a $2,000 approximate price increase. And what's crazy is looking at the prior 10 years from 1994 to 2004. There was another 25% or so price increase!

As you can see, the funeral business has experienced massive price increases. And it's just like everything else. Nothing is getting cheaper. I keep saying that, but it's true!

What's the point with this discussion? Hopefully, you can see how important it is to consider the long term. You must make sure you have enough final expense whole life insurance coverage.

As I said, $8,500 is the average cost today. But, what happens to pricing in 20 or 30 years?

Final Expense Whole Life Insurance – What NOT To Get

Understanding your options for final expense whole life insurance is very important. You do NOT want to make the wrong decision!

I've met more than 3,000 people since 2011 to discuss final expense whole life insurance, and work with final expense insurance agents in my agency nationally. Most I see are on a fixed income. And they all drowning in junk mail advertisements about final expense coverage.

I can't even get through a meeting with many of these people without seeing some advertisement for funeral expense insurance on TV!

And, if you're like most people, with the ever-increasing flyers and promotions regarding final expense coverage you receive you end up getting confused.

What I want to do is cover what is NOT final expense whole life insurance. It's very important to know the difference between good and bad coverage. Then, we'll define the basics of what is final expense whole life insurance.

1. Term Insurance

The first final expense insurance plan to stay away from is called term life insurance.

This is critical! If take away anything from this, it's that "term" is short for terminates. Literally, when you buy a term policy, you're betting you're going to die before the plan expires!

Did you catch that? Term plans expire, they terminate, they cancel! And many of the brand name insurance carriers you see through the mail and on TV offer ONLY term insurance. And in many cases, they are designed to terminate at 80 years old!

So, you could buy term insurance today, live an average length of life, then lose your coverage. That's crazy!

And it gets worse. Your premium rates go up with many of these plans. There are incremental increases every 5 years. So while it may be affordable at 60, will it be at 65, at 70, and again at 75?

Many times, it's not. And I would say most people end up dropping their coverage! Why? Because they just simply can't afford it anymore. They've paid all these years for it. But Social Security raises simply can't keep pace with the premium increases.

Sadly, many end up dropping it. It's a position you don't want to be in!

Sad Fact – we don't know when we're going to die. It could be tomorrow. Or 30 years from now. Therefore, we need to have a final expense plan that's guaranteed to pay under any circumstance.

It's important to have a guaranteed plan in place, because without it you are taking a risk. You're gambling!

The one positive aspect of term insurance is it's cheaper to start with. But, you get what you pay for.

Simply put, you pay less now for term insurance. BUT you'll pay a whole lot more later!

If you're on a fixed income, you get one check a month. Everything must fit that check. You must pinch pennies. You must watch everything that you buy.

Now imagine getting a price increase on your life insurance that doubles. It started off at $50, and now it's $100. Could you afford that?

You're going to have other expenses that go up in price, so why take that risk when you don't have to? This is why I do not like people who want final expense coverage to take out a term policy.

It's not that I'm against term insurance. It just depends on the circumstances. And the vast majority of people who want a guaranteed whole life insurance policy don't need to get a term policy.

2. Universal Life

Also included in insurance plans not to buy is Universal Life coverage.

Now, here's the deal. It's not always the case that Universal Life is a bad final expense policy. It's just something you should be wary of. You need to do your due diligence before you decide to buy it.

Sometimes, universal life insurance is really good. Sometimes it's the best choice! But, sometimes it's not. Let me explain.

Universal life insurance is not necessarily final expense whole life insurance. Sometimes Universal Life plans can be designed to last only to a particular age.

Many times, they'll last until 80, 85, or 90 years of age. So, in essence, universal life plans can operate as a term insurance policy. They have a limit of coverage. So, if you outlive that plan, then you lose your coverage, or the price substantially increases.

You have to ask yourself, what if you live to 100? You're still going to have final expenses after all! And you must seriously consider you're not really getting something that gives you a full lifetime guarantee.

Universal life insurance may not have guaranteed level premiums. You can get Universal Life programs with guaranteed premiums, and that's what you should do, assuming you find universal life insurance appropriate for your life insurance goals.

However, some agents will design these plans so there will be a price increase. We've seen it out in the field working with people face to face. Agents have come in and offered these Universal Life plans, and the client has kept it for decades.

Then, when they're in their 70s, they get this massive price increase letter. Sadly, they can't afford it anymore. They are understandably livid! And it's because the agent designed the plan from the outset in a way that was destined to fail.

It was going to be a long time before it did, but eventually it did. I'm not saying that Universal Life is not an option under any circumstances. But, it's a risk under certain circumstances.

You want to make sure you're working with an agent that fully understands Universal Life plans, how they work, and what they're doing for you. Have them explain to you what the guarantees are before you buy one of those plans.

What Type Of Final Expense Whole Life Insurance You SHOULD Get

We've talked about what not to get. Now let's cover what you should absolutely have in a whole life final expense program.

The following are the basics that should be included with every single final expense whole life insurance program. Maybe you're looking at something that looks like whole life called permanent insurance. Sometimes it's interchangeable terminology. But, you want to make sure you have these particular elements in your plan to ensure you're getting the best overall value.

1. Guaranteed Fixed Premium

First, make sure you have a guaranteed fixed premium for life.

One of the biggest advantages of a final expense whole life plan is that the premium stays the same. You do not have to worry about getting that dreaded price increase letter 5 years down the road.

Additionally, what you pay today is what you pay until you die. And that's great for someone on a fixed income.

There's no risk about not being able to afford a price increase. You can depend upon the price staying the same. It is a guaranteed must-have with any final expense whole life insurance plan.

2. Will Not Cancel

The second element of a final expense whole life insurance plan is it is guaranteed not to cancel due to health or age.

This is very important! I teach my clients to match the life insurance product with the particular problem she's trying to solve. Remember, all life insurance does is solves problems. And there are different problems for different people.

If you're a young man working hard, and you suddenly die, your wife is now in a perilous position to replace your income. It's really important to own a plan that covers in that circumstance.

For this situation, the perfect plan for that situation is term insurance. Why? Because it's the cheapest way to get coverage. If the man dies before the plan expires, his wife has all this money I would have earned if I had lived.

We're all going to die. And unfortunately, it can happen at any age. There are guaranteed expenses that will occur. And we don't want a plan that will expire before we do.

Think about it. Where is the logic in that? Why would I pay for a plan I might outlive it?

This is why your final expense whole life policy should be guaranteed not to cancel because of age or health.

3. Death Benefits Do Not Decrease

Third, you want to have a level death benefit that does not decrease.

I've seen decreasing death benefit life insurance plans. And when they hit a certain age, they decrease in coverage. But stay the same in price!

When it comes to final expense whole life insurance, what you see is what you get. You want a plan that covers you. Also, you want a plan that doesn't cancel because you're too old or because your health is bad. Plus, you want your plan to stay the same price from start to finish.

It's pretty simple. You don't want anything more complicated than that!

4. First-day 100% Coverage

Lastly, you want to try to get first-day 100% full coverage.

As I mentioned earlier, you're swimming through a boatload of junk mail and TV ads for final expense whole life insurance advertisements. Unfortunately, most of them make you wait 2 years before you're fully covered for natural death!

While you may get a brand-name company, what does it matter if you die from a natural cause like a stroke or cancer? If you die within those first 2 years on any of these plans, you're out of luck!

You don't want to get any of those plans if you don't have to.

Here's A Secret: work with an independent agent.

I'm an independent final expense whole life insurance agent. And I have since starting because I felt it was critical for me to shop the different carriers for the best insurance for my clients like you.

Many agents work for only one company. They only offer one product and one choice. And in many cases, it's just not the best choice for you. You're going to be overcharged and get inferior coverage. The short of it is it's not going to give you the best value that you deserve.

An independent agent works with many companies. For each of my clients, I figure out which company is going to be the best price and the best value of coverage. My goal is to get you 100% coverage for natural and accidental death from the first payment date.

That's my goal when I go out in the field and work with my clients. And that's what you deserve.

Agents that only offer products from one company have a limitation on underwriting. They won't be able to give you the best price. And in many cases, your health issues may completely disqualify you.

Therefore, it's critical you work with a final expense whole life insurance agent who is independent. They shop a variety of carriers and typically offer better underwriting, better pricing, and the outcome typically is better for you.

At the end of the day, you have to live with this plan. And if you're on a fixed income, you have to use every single dollar to the best of your ability. As you know, this means making sure you're not paying more than you have to. An independent agent is much more likely be able to do that.

Does Your Health Disqualify You For Final Expense Whole Life Insurance?

You may be thinking, "I've already been declined." This is a concern for everyone interested in a final expense whole life policy.

Luckily, health is usually not usually an obstacle to being qualified. Now, it does affect what you qualify for. But it's not something that will just fully disqualify you even if you've been turned down before.

There are companies that will take you at preferred rates, even if you've been turned down by others. You may doubt this, but that's how this business is. If you've been in this business long enough as an agent, you understand what I mean. And that's why you've got to represent multiple carriers. Why? Because certain carriers take health issues that others won't.

The key here is working with an independent agent to get better price, better underwriting, better value, and better for you.

Let's talk about some common conditions you can get quality coverage for from an independent agent. I'm going to run through a list of what I usually see and give you some perspective on what's possible.

Diabetes

First is diabetes. A lot of people have diabetes. They wonder what kind of coverage they can get, if any at all.

I have plenty of people who have basic type-2 diabetes that they were diagnosed with as adults. I can get them preferred coverage, even if they use insulin or have diabetic complications.

Also, I've had a lot of people with diabetic neuropathy get coverage. In most cases, that's no big deal. You just have to know which companies work and which ones don't. Even those with type-1 diabetes that started very early in life can get coverage.

Lung Disease Like Copd Or Asthma

I also work with the companies that will provide first day full coverage for lung disease. A lot of people smoke their whole lives, like my mom. She would tell me when I was a kid, as she took a drag on her 20th cigarette of the day, "Dave, don't ever, ever start this horrible habit." She's quit since then, but it's tough.

If you have COPD or asthma or some other respiratory problem, you may be thinking no insurance company is going to touch you. There are companies that will give you first-day 100% coverage for lung disease under most circumstances. And that's something I can help you with.

Heart Disease

If you have a history of heart disease, you may be leery of what you can qualify for. Maybe you had a heart attack, a stroke, a stent, bypass, seizures, aneurysms, a pacemaker, or other conditions.

I'm here to tell you that, if you work with the right independent agent, as long as it has been a certain length of time since your diagnosis, you can get covered. I can tell you within a minute or two what your options are.

Liver And Kidney Problems

Some kidney and liver problems can qualify depending on the time since the original diagnosis and treatment. There are also options for full first-day coverage for neurological problems such as lupus, multiple sclerosis, and Parkinson's.

Many people think if they can get any coverage it will be a 2-year wait guaranteed issue policy, and in most circumstances, that's not the case.

Mental Health Issues Like Depression, Bipolar, Schizophrenia

There are also carriers that will cover mental health issues such as depression, bipolar, and schizophrenia. There are other major health issues that can be covered that I didn't mention. I just wanted to use a broad brush here for the most common issues.

Now, I'm not trying to pull the wool over your eyes. Sometimes the only option people have is guaranteed acceptance policies. These policies don't ask any health questions. Additionally, you only get full coverage after paying in for 2 years.

But I want to stress that this is the minority when dealing with me. I can get full first-day coverage for many different conditions. That is not a promise, however, and if I can't, I'll tell you that too.

Keep in mind, it's still good to get some kind of policy because you could very well live longer than 2 years. So you don't want to be stuck in a situation where you don't have anything!

Don't Wait!

If you've stuck with me this far, you're obviously concerned about getting coverage on yourself, your spouse or maybe your parents or children. Don't wait any longer!

Once you've found a person to work with and can trust, don't wait! Many people I see are "world-class procrastinators." Don't be that guy! All it takes is one health event to totally disqualify you from ever getting full coverage at a preferred rate.

Your health is at its best today. Age has a way of making things worse, after all, and you can get better coverage if you're healthy. Lock in the price now at a low rate and get your full coverage.

One of the first people I ever wrote a policy on got full preferred coverage. She called me a month or two after her first payment to tell me she had a heart attack. As you can imagine, she was worried about whether she would be able to keep her coverage. I was able to tell her that her coverage would be fine. We always think bad things happen to other people, but they happen to us too. That's why we have final expense whole life insurance.

Make Sure Your Final Expense Whole Life Insurance Stays Within Your Budget

Some coverage is better than no coverage! A lot of loving parents and especially grandparents would love to get enormous policies to leave behind for their kids or grandkids, but sometimes our budget just won't allow it.

Make sure that you're shopping for a plan that is actually going to accomplish your primary goal. Anything left over can be given to your family. Just be okay with not getting everything that you want but getting what you need.

Make sure the policy you buy is easily affordable. There's nothing worse, as an agent, to sell a policy to somebody and then see them cancel it 6 months down the road. That's a waste of your money.

I would much rather you not buy it and spend it on something fun, instead of buying it and dropping it in 6 months because you bought too much. Buying too much is just setting a landmine for later down the road when you can no longer afford it. Then you're back where you started with no coverage.

I work with my clients to make sure their policy is easily affordable. I've even talked people out of buying too much just because I don't want to see them potentially drop it. I certainly want to help people to the extent they want to be helped, and if it's affordable, it's that much easier to keep.

Use An Independent Agent When Shopping For Final Expense Whole Life Insurance

Finally, make sure your agent is independent. Always ask whoever you're dealing with if they're an independent agent and to let you see what companies they represent.

You want them to actually show you the applications and brochures to prove they work with multiple carriers. For example, if someone asked me for a brochure, I'll throw out all the brochures. I'll show them where I'm appointed, and I'll tell them about the companies. I'll go into detail about everything to give them the assurance that I'm independent and can shop around to get my client the best value.

Conclusion

I would be remiss if I didn't offer you my services if you're interested in qualifying for final expense whole life insurance.

If you are interested, I implore you to give me a call at 888-626-0439 or contact me from my website at buylifeinsuranceforburial.com for a free, no-obligation quote.

I am a very low-key, relaxed agent, and I only want to help you if you want help. I've been doing this since 2011, and I really care about my clients and making sure they get the best price and value.

If you decide to contact me, I'll ask you some health questions, figure out exactly where things stand, give you a couple prices within your budget, and then you decide if it makes sense for you.

If you just want to think about it, that's fine too. I'm not a high-pressure guy; I never have been. To be in this business, you have to have a servant's heart to help people.

3 SIX STEPS TO BUYING THE BEST FINAL EXPENSE INSURANCE POLICY

Final expense insurance – the one insurance product we KNOW we need! But often we put off.

And if you're like most of my clients, you see tons of junk mail and television ads offering final expense life insurance.

And that's why I'm writing this article for you. There is so much misinformation regarding final expense insurance. Even worse, many are unaware of the competitively-priced final expense insurance options available to them.

When it comes to the television and junk mail final expense insurance companies, most have "fine print gotcha" clauses that will cause you grief. In fact, many I talk to are convinced they cannot qualify for affordable, high quality final expense life insurance.

How To Get Affordable Final Expense Life Insurance?

Luckily, most people can qualify for excellent final expense insurance at great rates. All you need to know are the facts, so you can pick the best plan.

This article is designed to do just that! Since 2011, I've seen too many final expense insurance companies ripping off regular people. And what's shocking is that these rip-off final expense insurance options are name-brand companies you've heard of!

My goal is to give you the information necessary to empower yourself. By the end of this article, you'll know how to select the best final expense insurance plan. That way, your loved ones will not worry about paying for your burial, cremation, or any other final expenses.

Step 1: Final Expense Insurance Based Around Your NEEDS.

As a final expense insurance agent, my goal is to help people like you find a plan that actually does the job you want to accomplish. And, if you're like most, you're on a <u>fixed income</u>. Your budget only allows so much for a final expense insurance plan.

Therefore, when you buy a final expense life insurance plan, make sure it **meets your needs!**

And the first need is that it fits your budget.

First, do NOT let an insurance agent persuade you to spend more than you can afford. Instead, you MUST buy a plan it fits your budget.

Sometimes you're best served through starting with a lower-priced plan. Why? Because losing your final expense insurance policy is unfortunate. Which is why focusing on affordable first is crucial!

First, focus on working within your means. Know your budget. Also, keep in mind a premium that's easily affordable. Let *that* be your guiding light.

Step 2: What's The Best Final Expense Life Insurance – Term Or Whole?

Now, let me describe to you the difference between term life and whole life insurance.

Term life insurance is what we call "terminating insurance." Simply put, **term life insurance cancels at a future date**. And with most final expense insurance term products, 80 is the cancellation age. And since people living longer lives, many people who purchase term life insurance will outlive them. And not have final expense insurance... *exactly at the point they need it!*

Think about it. How would you feel if you lost your final expense insurance? Feels like you're getting ripped off, right?

Term Insurance Goes Up In Price AND Cancels, Too!

This is exactly what I tell my clients. And not only do term life insurance plans cancel, **they also go up in price, too!**

If final expense insurance is important to you to own, *then avoid term life insurance.* In most cases, it's not going to be there when you need it. And, if it is, it's usually too expensive to keep!

What's the solution? I recommend final expense whole life insurance.

Whole life insurance never cancels because of age or health, premiums never increase, and in many cases, you're fully approved and covered from the first day. Naturally, getting full-coverage final expense whole life insurance depends on answering a set of health-related questions. However, many people do qualify for full coverage. In most cases, this is the best kind of final expense whole life insurance plan to own.

Here's the takeaway: Do you plan on dying before or after 80? Don't know? None of us do!

If you feel the same way, final expense whole life insurance is best. Because it will be there no matter when pass. Without having ever-increasing premiums that you can't afford.

Step 3: The Truth Behind "Junk Mail" Final Expense Insurance.

Do you watch television? Are you receiving tons of junk mail daily? If so, I know you see all sorts of ads about final expense insurance.

Be careful with junk mail final expense insurance offers! Why be wary? Because the final expense companies do a superb job describing their final expense insurance. In some cases, these companies are known for bringing on celebrities for personal endorsements.

Unfortunately, these final expense companies use celebrity endorsements and fancy for a specific reason...

To DISTRACT You From The Final Expense Insurance "Fine Print!"

Want the "ugly" truth? Many of these final expense life insurance companies only offer a "guaranteed acceptance" policy that offers no coverage for two years!

Meaning, if you die within the first two years, your loved ones do NOT get the full payout!

Also, many of the final expense insurance policies are term insurance. As we described above, term insurance for final expense typically go up every 5 years and cancel at 80.

How do you get around this? You have to deal with what is known an independent agent. An independent agent shops different final expense whole life insurance companies. The goal is to get you the best price and value of coverage.

Even better, many of these agents have final expense whole life insurance policy offers you can't find anywhere else. And people are shocked at how much better of deal they get compared to the junk mail companies.

So deal with an independent agent. But make sure the agent isn't pushy, is someone you can trust, and is interested in helping you.

Step 4: Consider Working With An Independent Final Expense Insurance Broker, NOT A Captive Agent.

This is a great step all people considering final expense insurance should take. First, let me describe the difference.

A captive final expense insurance agent is beholden to one life insurance company. By definition, the captive agent can usually offer only one final expense insurance option. And in most cases, the option is neither the best price nor the best value in final expense life insurance coverage!

An independent final expense whole life insurance agent gives you multiple options. If they operate as I do, they carry about 15 different insurance companies. And once they ask the client the health questions, the independent final expense life insurance agent selects the best value for the client. And many times, issues like age and health aren't nearly as much of a factor in getting coverage.

More often than not, this leads to a better deal for you!

You typically get more final expense insurance coverage and a better premium. Plus, the experience is more positive. Whereas, if you get stuck with the one-trick pony final expense insurance agent, you're going to spend too much and not get the best coverage.

Ask yourself this. Would you prefer to get the best deal for final expense insurance? Or would you prefer to work with somebody who can't?

Most people want the best deal! So, working with an independent final expense whole life insurance agent is very important.

Step 5: How To Select The Best Final Expense Life Insurance Plan

This step relates to the first step. You want a final expense life insurance plan that meets your needs and covers all expenses.

Sometimes, the final expense insurance policies aren't going to be able to cover all of the final expenses. Why? Because most people in retirement are not made of money!

So, what do you do if you can't get a plan that covers everything? Think, "Something is better than nothing."

In my experience, no funeral home refused half of the money required to bury someone. And many times, funeral directors will work with you if you can come up with part of the payment. It's better to get some money than none, after all!

Step 6: How To Qualify For Final Expense Life Insurance With No Exam, And No Visit From A Salesperson.

Advancements in qualifying for final expense whole life insurance allows many get quality coverage without a visit from an insurance agent.

Many people nowadays are uncomfortable having a stranger visit. More so, people are just downright leery with the way the world is these days! And I certainly don't blame them.

I've sold final expense whole life insurance face to face my entire career. So I understand why some people have issues with face-to-face visits.

Get Final Expense Insurance Without A Visit From An Agent!

That's why I have developed the ability to help people over the phone without requiring a visit!

Here's the thing. If you deal with somebody over the phone, you want to make sure they're legitimate. This is the reason why I wrote this article for you. I want to demonstrate my knowledge to you about the final expense programs available to you. I want to show you it is possible to get quality final expense life insurance, without spending a lot of money. And do it in a way that's convenient for you.

I now specialize in helping people without seeing them face to face in many states across the nation. Odds are, if you're reading this, I'm licensed in your state and can help you out.

If you're interested to see how the process actually works, all you have to do is complete a simple application. Most of the time this can be done over the phone. And no medical exams are required, too. The final expense insurance company will run your records, and your final expense insurance policy usually gets approved right on the spot. Most of the time there is zero paperwork! It is a great way to get a good, quality, affordable final expense life insurance plan without spending a lot of money.

Next Steps To Getting Affordable Final Expense Insurance

So how do you actually get more information on what your options are? Since everyone's health is different and states have different companies, the best thing you can do is to call me at 888-626-0439. Or, go to buylifeinsuranceforburial.com/contact/ to send a message. We'll get back to you with more information about what your options are for coverage. Make sure you fill the form out completely. That will help us to better prepare for speaking with you to get you the final expense insurance plan that works best for you.

4 MINI TOPICS RELATED TO FINAL EXPENSE INSURANCE

No Questions Asked Life Insurance – What's The Catch?

I'm a life insurance agent who works with people 50 and older. In the course of business, I'm often asked about these life insurance ads people get in their junk mail.

People wonder what these programs are all about and are usually rather skeptical. In reality, you should be skeptical about how these no questions asked life insurance plans really work.

The truth is these policies have a two-year waiting period for natural death causes. This means, if you die from cancer or heart issues, they will not pay the full death benefit. Unfortunately, I know several people who died literally days before the two years were up who were left with no coverage.

What's really sad is there are so many options out there to get coverage, even while battling diabetes, COPD, cancer history, heart history, and all sorts of other issues.

In conclusion, don't go with a no questions asked life insurance plan until you have looked at all other options. Furthermore, you should talk with an independent agent. He will shop around to see if he can get you the best deal. Fortunately, that's what I do at buylifeinsuranceforburial.com.

Best Burial Insurance For The Elderly

I want to give you the resources to determine the best insurance for somebody in their senior years. When we say senior years, we mean somebody who's typically 60 and older.

What Is Final Expense Insurance?

The first thing that I always ask my clients is, "What do you want your policy to do for you?" Most people --I'd say 90% of them-- want to pay for final expenses.

So what are final expenses? Final expenses consist of burial costs, cremation costs, any kind of final expenses that they don't necessarily want or can't pay out of savings. A final expense policy can do that so that children and beneficiaries don't have to.

What kind of policy is best for a senior who's looking for life insurance? It depends on what you want. Most people --because they want to guarantee something will be there no matter when they pass away-- are looking for policies that have guarantees on price, guarantees on coverage, and that will hopefully cover them from the first day. By that very definition, most people DO NOT want term insurance.

What Is Term Insurance?

Term insurance is short for terminating insurance or temporary insurance. It's very good --some of the most affordable coverage to buy-- but the problem with term insurance is that it ends at a certain point.

For example, if you need to ensure the mortgage gets paid if you die unexpectedly, term insurance makes perfect sense. But if you're looking to cover a cremation, a burial, or any other final expenses, why would you want a policy that is temporary in nature?

What Is Whole Life Final Expense?

That's why I recommend what's called a whole life final expense plan as the best life insurance for elderly. They range from as small as a couple thousand dollars all the way up to a $100,000. It just depends on the need of the client.

The rates of the policies never increase --usually they're locked in for life. Otherwise, you pay on the policy for a certain number of years. Then you stop paying and you own the insurance like you own your car after you pay off your car loan.

Also, the coverage never cancels because of age or health. The great thing is that we can usually find insurance that will cover my clients with first-day 100% coverage even if they have a history of health problems. I can't guarantee it, of course. But because I shop around for the best carriers, I can usually find the best deals for my clients.

To sum up, to get first-day coverage regardless of your health, you should find a whole life final expense plan.

Best Burial Insurance For People Between 86 And 90 Years Old

I wrote this post because most companies don't offer coverage past the age of 85. Meaning the moment you turn 86, 99% of companies cut you off from getting coverage.

This includes companies such as the ones you see commercials on TV for and receive junk mail from. However, if you're in that situation where you're 86 years old or older and you're looking for some kind of policy to pay for your final expenses --don't worry there are plans available for you that I can help you with.

If you're looking for something affordable that will cover you from the first day, you do have options if your health fits.

Independent Agent v. Captive Agent

I work with numerous life insurance companies. There are several that will offer you burial insurance even after you turn 86 depending on your health, of course. This is one of the benefits of working with an independent agent rather than with a captive agent.

Best Burial Insurance For People Between 50 And 60 Years Old

When it comes to final expense coverage, most of the people we sell to are 50 to 90 years old. So the 50 to 60-year-old crowd is a little bit different than the older people as far as health goes. Therefore, there are differences in which is the best plan for you and which plans to stay away from.

Better Health

The number one thing I can suggest is typically with a younger age comes better-than-average health. So it's always good to work with somebody who has competitive companies that will give you the better price.

There are a lot of carriers out there that actually have very high prices that are unnecessary for people 50 to 60 years old. You want to work with an agent, like myself, that works with many companies and will shop around to find you the best deal. That's number one.

Different Goals

Number two, you want to make sure that whatever plan you pick fits the goal you want to accomplish. So if your main goal is to have just enough insurance to cover a burial, make sure you get what I call a whole life plan. A whole life plan never cancels, never goes up in price, is locked in place, and hopefully has first-day coverage.

What you want to stay away from in most cases is term insurance. Term insurance terminates after a period of time. Meaning it can go away before you do, and it goes up in price. You've got to be very wary of that and make sure you stay away from those kinds of plans if your goal is to keep a plan for the rest of your life.

How To Get Life Insurance For Your Parents

If you're in your 30s, 40s, or maybe even older and you're looking for some kind of life insurance that would be the best value for your parents, I'd like you to check out my website. I'm a licensed broker. That means I represent different companies, so I can shop around to find the best price and coverage for you.

As an agent, I have a lot of experience selling to people 60 and older who need just enough to bury or cremate them and maybe leave some money behind. I've got some pretty strong opinions on what to look for and what to stay away from.

What To Stay Away From

First of all, you want to stay away from anything that comes through the mail. Generally speaking, the big-name companies tend to be the worst in this marketplace --AARP, Colonial Penn, MetLife, Globe. If you see it on TV or get it in the mail, chances are it doesn't offer the best deal.

Colonial Penn, MetLife, and Mutual of Omaha have a 2-year waiting period if the person dies by natural causes. So if your parent has a stroke in the first 2 years of the policy, then they don't pay the full death claim. They try to hide that from you, and they're very good at that actually. Most people don't realize it until it's too late, unfortunately. If you get AARP or Globe, your insurance may increase in price and then cancel at age 80.

What To Look For

My whole point is that these are reputable companies, but the products are just garbage. The best thing you can do if you're looking for affordable life insurance for your parents is to talk to a broker like myself. As a representative of multiple companies, my job is to find you the best price and the best coverage.

Most of what I sell is called whole life insurance. I can sell other kinds, but most people just want enough to bury them. Whole life is a much better deal for a variety of reasons.

Never Buy Term Life Insurance For Final Expense Coverage - Here's Why

In my opinion, term insurance for final expense is not a good idea. You have to understand first what term means. A simple way to remember what term insurance means is that term terminates. This means when you hit a certain age the policy ceases to exist. It cancels, it's done, and you have no coverage.

The question I ask my clients when they're looking for some kind of plan to pay for their burial is, do you want a plan that you may outlive? Or more succinctly, do you know when you're going to die? Of course, everybody says, "No, I don't know when I am going to die, and I don't want to outlive my coverage." If that's the way you answer, then it's highly likely that you don't want a term insurance policy.

What Else Is There?

Now, why would somebody consider them? Because they're very inexpensive relative to what's called whole life insurance. Whole life, however, is the opposite of term. It never cancels because of age, the rates never go up, and the coverage, in many cases if you work with an independent agent such as myself, can start from the first day. Sometimes we can only partially cover you, but in many cases, you can be fully covered. It's not a guarantee, but many times we can do it.

The point is that the nature of our death is uncertain. I don't know when I'm going to die. I'm 31 years old. I may pass away before you do even if you're in your 50's, 60's, or 70's. The fact of the matter is we need a plan that we will never outlive, that will be there no matter when the time comes.

5 BEST BURIAL INSURANCE FOR MEMORY DISORDERS

The truth is it's next to impossible to get anything with some sort of memory disorder. Most memory disorders are classified as either Alzheimer's or dementia. This is where you lose some of your short-term and even your long-term memory capability.

Unfortunately, there is no better choice for life insurance other than a guaranteed issue plan. What that means is this. Most companies won't talk to you if you take Aricept or Namenda, or any other cognitive memory treatment medication.

However, you can get a plan. The catch is that anybody that has any of those is going to have limited coverage for two years.

This means if you pass from natural causes, your beneficiary receives interest plus the money paid in. However, if you live past the waiting period, the policy pays out entirely. This means you have to live greater than 2 years before full coverage takes effect.

I'm mentioning this is because you do have options. If you've talked to an agent before and got declined, please call. It's very simple. I have carriers that can get you coverage with those issues. I shop around to find the best burial insurance prices. That way, you benefit by paying the least amount possible.

6 BEST BURIAL INSURANCE FOR CANCER HISTORY

Let me give you a little background on what I mean when I say cancer and then give you some options that you do have. First, whether you can qualify depends on if you currently have cancer or if it's been some time. There are options for each stage, and I'm going to go into detail about what those options are.

First of all, what exactly do I mean when I say cancer? When I say cancer, it really means the typical type of cancer you think of that can move around the body and infect different areas of the body. For example, if you get basal cell skin carcinoma, that's not the kind of cancer we're talking about. You actually qualify for good full coverage at a preferred price with that type of cancer.

Now, if you have what most people think of as cancer, such as lung cancer, prostate cancer, and so forth, the type of plan you qualify for is based on time. How long have you had cancer? When did you stop treatment? When was your last procedure? Let's break that down.

You Have Cancer Currently.

If you currently have cancer, your best option is a guaranteed issue plan. Guaranteed issue gets you approved for a plan but doesn't fully cover you for natural causes. This means, if you die from cancer within the first two years of most guaranteed issue plans, they only refund the money you paid in plus a nominal level of interest. The flip side to that is, if you do live past two years, it will pay the full amount. No questions asked even if you had cancer at the time you took the policy out. One good thing about that plan is you are covered 100% from the first day for accidental causes of death as described in the policy.

Cancer-Free For A Year Or More

Now, let's say you've been cancer-free for more than a year. At that point, you may qualify for a graded life insurance plan. Simply put, graded life insurance means is that you get partial coverage from the very first day. Meaning if you died within the next day or two after the policy is effective, then they will pay out a portion of the face amount of the policy.

This portion is usually between 30% and 45%. If you bought a $10,000 policy, you would get a payout somewhere between $3,000 and $4,500 depending on how the policy actually reads and what grade it is specifically defined by. A 30% payout is far better than nothing. Most companies make you wait two, three, or even four years before they'll talk to you if you've had cancer. This is a good option to get something on the books once you are cancer-free for more than a year.

Cancer-Free For 2+ Years

What if you're looking at two years or maybe even three years out from treatment and cancer? There's a lot of options that will give you first day 100% coverage. You want to take advantage of that as quickly as possible. It's not hard to get. You just need to talk to somebody like myself who brokers for different companies and can get you qualified for a plan.

7 BEST BURIAL INSURANCE FOR DEPRESSION, BIPOLAR, AND SCHIZOPHRENIA

First of all, when I say a mental health issue, it can range from something as minor as depression or bipolar to something as highly problematic and medicated as schizophrenia. These are the primary three mental health issues I'm talking about. As many people know, you can often operate without any problems as long as you're properly medicated. The good news is that most of these companies recognize that.

Depression

For depression, it's very simple to get you first-day coverage regardless of the type of depression. It's okay. It's very simple to get, and I deal with it every day.

Bipolar

Bipolar is somewhat harder, but I have access to companies that will be more than happy to work with you. I have clients that have been treated with medication as strong as lithium for bipolar disorder. We can get you coverage. It is not a problem at all.

Schizophrenia

The last issue is schizophrenia. Schizophrenia, I'm happy to report, is very simple to get qualified for, even if you've had it your entire life. Many people can stay medicated and be fine, and we can get you coverage where many agents can't.

8 BEST BURIAL INSURANCE FOR CARDIAC ISSUES

Many think heart disease health issues eliminate burial insurance eligibility. Luckily, this is not the case! With enough time passed since the health even, you'll have plenty of opportunities to purchase quality life insurance for final expenses. Let's break it down.

Heart Attack, Stroke, Stents, Bypass, Aneurysms, Pacemaker History Within The Past 12 Months

If you've had a heart attack, stroke, stent implant, open-heart bypass, aneurysm, or pacemaker implant within the last 12 months, a guaranteed-issue final expense plan is your best life insurance option.

What Is Guaranteed Issue Life Insurance?

Guaranteed issue life insurance is designed to approve coverage, no matter the applicant's health. However, if you pass away from natural causes, guaranteed issue life insurance limits the death benefit for the first two years.

So, while you're covered fully for accidental death, any natural cause of death - related to heart disease or not - will not give your beneficiaries a full death-benefit payout.

Why Would I Want To Get A Plan Like That?

When a guaranteed-issue life insurance plan is all my client can qualify for, they routinely ask, "Why even bother with a burial insurance plan that doesn't cover from the first day?" So, here's why I recommend buying a guaranteed issue final expense insurance plan. Despite NOT having full first-day natural death coverage.

Your Health Could Change At Any Moment

Here's the truth. You could have another heart attack, or heart-related health crisis.
You could develop a new disease like diabetes. Or your doctor may prescribe you a new medication.

Why does this matter? Because ALL future health events may prevent you from qualifying for quality life insurance for final expenses. If you wait for better options for burial insurance coverage, negative changes in your health will eliminate qualifying for anything better.

Bottom line - this means you may STILL have to wait two years before your natural death coverage begins… when you COULD have been fully covered. IF you took the final expense coverage out earlier on!

Hopefully this makes sense!

Thankfully, nearly all my clients with heart-health issues understand this. And ultimately, they purchase a guaranteed-issue plan. Why? My clients clearly understand waiting any longer to get covered is a gamble.

Heart Attack, Stroke, Stents, Bypass, Aneurysms, Pacemaker History Within The Past 1 To 2 Years

Have you had a heart-related health event in the past 12 to 24 months? If so, you may qualify for a few good final expense insurance options.

For example, you may qualify for "standard," first-day, 100% coverage policy, or a "graded" plan, which partially covers you from the first day of purchasing the burial insurance policy. Not every agent offers these plans. However, final expense insurance brokers like myself do!

Feel free to call or message me if you fit this situation. I'm happy to help.

Heart Attack, Stroke, Stents, Bypass, Aneurysms, Pacemaker History - 2 Years Or Greater Since The Event Took Place

If you're heart or circulatory event occurred two years or greater, you may qualify for full, first-day final expense coverage. In fact, many final expense companies will consider you at preferred pricing!

Nevertheless, there are several implications to consider prior to ensuring your preferred pricing qualification.

For example, do you take blood thinners, such as Coumadin, Warfarin, or Plavix?

Do you also take isosorbide, or Nitroglycerin? While some burial insurance companies accept these prescriptions, many do not.

Again, work with a final expense broker like myself. Brokers navigate the options to provide the best insurance options, unique to your individual case.

What Cardiac And Heart Health Issues Are ALWAYS Considered Guaranteed-Issue Life Insurance?

Unfortunately, some cardiac heart history issues can never qualify for first day full coverage. Let's detail those conditions below.

Congestive Heart Failure And Burial Insurance

Congestive heart failure causes water to pool around the heart. It's an extremely serious cardiac condition and never entirely goes away. Unfortunately, almost all final expense carriers offer only a guaranteed-issue option.

However, one final expense carrier may qualify you for "graded," partial first-day coverage. Despite the potential, my experience is few end up qualifying for coverage, as there are additional health questions that prevent the applicant from qualifying.

Angina, Nitroglycerin Usage For Final Expense Insurance

If you are prescribing nitroglycerin, isosorbide mononitrate, or have an angina diagnosis, you'll have more difficulty qualifying for a first-day full coverage final expense policy.

With many burial insurance carriers, nitrate medications are an automatic decline. At best, the carriers will offer a two-year waiting period, guaranteed-issue option. Now, this isn't case with all carriers. However, I prepare my clients to expect it.

Angina is in the same boat, as nitrates treat angina.

Other Cardiac And Circulatory Diseases

Moving on, let's look at other cardiac and circulatory health issues that surprisingly can qualify for quality life insurance.

Seizure History

Some insurance companies decline individuals a history of seizures, or prescriptions to prevent seizures. However, may insurance carriers I work with are lenient with both a history of seizures and seizure-preventative medications.

For example, medications such as Keppra or Dilantin qualify with many companies as first-day full coverage at preferred rates! Even better, a few select companies exist that accept applicants with a recent history of seizure events, as well.

As in all situations, qualification comes down to the applicant's total health picture. But understand this. It is possible to get somebody with recent seizures, or someone who takes seizure-preventative medications, first-day full coverage.

Please contact me and I'll see what I can do to help you.

Pacemakers And Life Insurance

Most insurance carriers qualify pacemaker installations as a cardiac surgery event, similar to heart attack or stroke history. However, a few carriers will allow first-day full coverage for pacemaker patients that have passed more than 12 months since the installation.

Have you recently had a battery change on our pacemaker? If so, you may qualify for preferred, first-day full coverage, since many companies do not treat battery changes as cardiac events.

Diabetes With Heart Disease History

Some carriers look negatively at applicants with a diabetes diagnosis in combination with a heart or circulatory history. Why? Studies have shown that diabetes exacerbates and worsens the likelihood of cardiac health history issues. Therefore, insurance carrier underwriters at some carriers will rate up the cost of your final expense coverage.

Here's the good news. I shop the major final expense carriers to see who offers you the best burial insurance option. And many times, I find options that don't care about a combination of heart history and diabetic issues.

9 BEST BURIAL INSURANCE FOR DIABETES

Since becoming licensed to sell final expense insurance in 2011, I've met countless people who think a diabetes diagnosis severely limits life insurance coverage options.

Luckily, I have good news! When working with the right final expense insurance agent, you'll have plenty of high-quality final expense insurance options, despite the diabetes diagnosis. Ultimately, the key is to work with a broker. He can shop the most competitively priced and highest quality carriers on the market.

Diagnosed With Diabetes And Only Taking Pills Or Managed With Diet

Most people who have diabetes only take pills. And, many that have a diagnosis of diabetes who manage their food intake can control the disease with no medication whatsoever.

Here's the good news. If this is the only form of diabetes you have, your options for final expense coverage are fantastic! Thankfully, most insurance companies are flexible with a basic diabetic diagnosis.

In summary, rest assured that you can qualify for high-quality final expense coverage, as long as your diabetes is under control with pills or diet.

Diabetes Managed With Insulin

This is where things get a little tricky. Many insurance companies will cover somebody who has insulin use. However, there's a few circumstances to overcome first in order to find the right company to work with.

Did You Start Insulin After The Age Of 50?

If you started the insulin after turning 50, you should qualify for most final expense Insurance options. Simply put, the goal is to find the company with the best rate and value.

Did You Start Insulin In Your 40s?

Starting insulin in your 40s is younger than most diabetics start taking insulin. Luckily, we're able to get you quality final expense insurance without any issues if you started insulin in your 40s.

Are You A Type 1 Diabetic?

Type 1 diabetics are diabetics diagnosed in childhood. Typically, Type 1 diabetics use insulin before 10 years old or slightly thereafter. Historically, Type 1 Diabetics have had difficulty getting quality coverage. However, it is now possible to get final expense insurance, despite a Type 1 Diabetic diagnosis.

Ultimately, the key is to work with an agent that can shop the best carriers. That's where we come in.

Complications Of Diabetes

Folks with complications of diabetes can be challenging to insure. First, there's several circumstances to consider.

Diabetic Neuropathy

When a diabetic begins to develop pain in the feet, legs, and hands, many times diabetic neuropathy is to blame.

Truth be told, many have hard times qualifying for full coverage with a diabetic neuropathy diagnosis. However, we have access to carriers that approve folks with diabetic neuropathy with quality final expense coverage. Give us a call for more information.

Nephropathy And Amputations Due To Diabetes

These conditions are more challenging to cover. First, nephropathy is the outcome of diabetes as it affects the kidneys. And, amputations are the outcome of uncontrolled diabetes.

Thankfully, we still can help you out. We'll need to ask you some more specific questions to figure out what your options are.

10 BEST BURIAL INSURANCE FOR KIDNEY ISSUES

Kidney problems are a tough issue to deal with in the final expense life insurance market, but it is possible to get good coverage at an affordable rate, under certain circumstance. So I'm going to list a few different situations defined as kidney problems and then go into your options.

The most common kidney problem we see is end-stage renal failure requiring dialysis. This means your kidneys cannot function alone, and you require the assistance of a dialysis clinic three days a week. At the clinic, they clean and process your blood to keep you healthy. In fact, without it you will die.

End-stage renal disease is a terminal condition, and unfortunately, there are no companies that will provide first-day coverage. Pretty much the only option you have is what we call a two-year waiting period policy. That means you have to wait for two years after you take out the policy before you're fully covered.

If you die by accident, then you get 100% coverage from the first day you took the plan out. But understand that for natural death, such as kidney disease, there are no options. It's always a two-year wait. I've worked in this business for a very long time, talked to dozens of dialysis patients and insurance companies. There are no other options besides that.

End-stage kidney failure without dialysis is where things get interesting. There are preliminary stages to dialysis. That's why it's called end-stage because there are stages in between. If you have kidney problems such that your kidney function deteriorates but your body still functions, we've got options for you. There are several companies that will give you full 100% coverage, if not graded coverage, under certain circumstances if you have kidney problems but not complete and total failure.

It depends on a couple of factors-- medication usage and other health history. But it's very hard to find good coverage for this particular issue. If you end-stage renal disease, you are honestly looking at the possibility of dialysis in the future. So you want to lock in a good policy that gets you coverage from the first day.

Now, the other situation is if you have had a kidney transplant. If you've ever had an organ transplant, no matter if it's a kidney or not, your only option is going to be a two-year wait. There's no way around that, unfortunately. You're on anti-rejection medications the rest of your life. The truth is that an organ transplant is not guaranteed to work out. So if you are in that situation, understand that the best thing to do is lock in a good price on a good two-year waiting period product, like a Gerber's product.

11 BEST BURIAL INSURANCE FOR RESPIRATORY ISSUES

Chronic lung problems are some of the hardest issues to cover when it comes to final expense burial insurance.

Chronic Respiratory Disease

Most companies in the burial insurance business lump all chronic disorders together. For example, chronic obstructive pulmonary disease, emphysema, tuberculosis history, chronic bronchitis are all considered as the same severity. This applies basically to any issues requiring ongoing treatment with inhalers using medications such as Spiriva, Advair, Proair or oxygen usage.

COPD

Fortunately, as medications improve, more companies are allowing people with COPD to get full first-day coverage under certain conditions. There are actually several companies that provide 100% coverage for smokers, which is fantastic!

The only exception to this rule is if there are a lot of issues in conjunction with COPD. For example, very bad diabetes, very recent heart problems or more severe cases of COPD requiring 24/7 oxygen usage can make it tougher. Oxygen usage tends to be a chronic issue that never goes away. Therefore, there are very, very few companies that will give first-day full coverage to people using oxygen.

However, that doesn't mean you can't get coverage. It just means it's that much harder. If you are on oxygen, your best bet is a two-year waiting period product. This means you have to wait two years before coverage for natural death kicks in. You receive 100% coverage for accidental death, but not natural causes.

What Can You Do?

So I write all this to advise you that you have limited choices if you are on oxygen. But we can get you coverage that's affordable if you will work with an independent agent, like myself, to shop around and get you the best deal.

There are the rare occasions where somebody has COPD but doesn't need any sort of ongoing treatment. Therefore, they don't have any medical history of prescriptions being filled within the past several years.

If you fit this category, it is very possible to find you first-day coverage at preferred rates. While this is the exception to the rule, I can sometimes measurably improve coverage for people normally limited to a higher-priced plan or a two-year waiting product.

12 BEST BURIAL INSURANCE FOR HIV AND AIDS PATIENTS

Since 2011, I've meet a number of people with AIDS and HIV diagnoses. Historically, life insurance carriers have made it difficult to approve final expense life insurance for folks with these conditions.

Good news! Despite HIV and AIDS diagnoses, it's easier than ever to qualify for affordable life insurance protection, designed to take care of final expenses and replace income.

Options For Final Expense Coverage With An HIV Positive Diagnosis

In late 2015, several carriers rolled out new final expense life insurance developments for HIV positive patients. Specifically, these insurance companies introduced coverage to quality HIV positive patients for high-quality life insurance.

Currently, if you are HIV positive, and your age is between 30 and 60, you may qualify for a 10- or 15-year term insurance product with a major life insurance company.

Below, you'll find more information on how to qualify for these 10 or 15-year term life insurance products:

- Life insurance coverage limit is $2,500,000.00
- Applicant must be a U.S. Resident.
- Medical underwriting guidelines are as follows:
- HIV cannot originate from intravenous drug use.
- You cannot have Hepatitis B or Hepatitis C history.
- No Tuberculosis, and nontuberculous abacterial infection
- HIV diagnosis greater than 12 months in length.
- 6 months or longer since beginning antiretroviral therapy.
- Current CD4 count less than 350, and done within the last 6 months
- Lowest CD4 count greater than 200, and no history of an AIDS defining illness.

Final Expense Life Insurance For AIDS Diagnosis

Many reading this may have an AIDS diagnosis, and wonder what they qualify for. While AIDS patients can now qualify for final expense coverage, the programs differ than those offered to HIV-positive patients. Read below to find out more.

No Questions Asked Life Insurance For AIDS Patients

As of publishing this article, no questions-asked life insurance is the the only options for folks testing positive for AIDS.

No questions asked life insurance is fairly self-explanatory. The applicant purchases the policy without answering any health questions. And this includes questions about AIDS.

Pros And Cons Of No-Questions Asked Life Insurance

Here are the benefits to a no-questions asked life insurance program:

- You don't have to take a medical exam
- You don't have to answer health questions
- Coverage cannot be declined, assuming you fit the age requirements.

Essentially, if you can sign your name, you're approved!

Here are the drawbacks to no-questions asked life insurance for final expenses:

- Death from natural causes limited for the for the first two years.

Bottom line, if you pass away from any natural causes, your beneficiary receives premiums refunded, plus ten percent interest (some more, some less).

Keep in mind this includes any natural causes of death. And while I much prefer covering my clients fully for natural death, my clients with an AIDS diagnosis leaves us this only option.

Think Long-Term

Why you buy final expense life insurance if you're not covered immediately?

First, starting coverage sooner gets you to full coverage faster. Imagine putting off buying final expense life insurance because you are frustrated you cannot get full coverage.

Regardless of your frustration, you'll have to wait two full years for natural death coverage. So, you're putting off the inevitable. And putting your family at risk! I have several clients who passed away after the two-year waiting. If they did not have the coverage, their families would have gone broke funding their funeral and final expenses.

I am thankful for new advances in coverage options for AIDS and HIV clients. Thankfully, you can get quality final expense life insurance much easier than before.

13 BEST BURIAL INSURANCE FOR NEUROLOGICAL DISORDERS

To start, I define neurological disorders as issues such as Parkinson's, multiple sclerosis, Lou Gehrig's disease, and other issues that affect the nervous system. Usually people have had these issues for years. There are no cures. Sometimes they're manageable. Other times they're not.

Parkinson's

For example, Parkinson's is manageable, and most insurance companies out there know that. Therefore, they are either going to give you first-day partial or full coverage. I try to get my clients full first-day coverage.

So if you have Parkinson's, please talk to me. I can give you a lot more options for life insurance coverage than a lot of other agents can.

Lou Gehrig's

If you have Lou Gehrig's disease, you may have options for full first-day coverage. Issues like lupus or multiple sclerosis also last forever but are manageable.

I can help you get full first-day coverage for either of those issues. It is possible. You just need to work with someone like me who can shop around for the best deal. Many of these companies on TV are not going to give you the best deal.

The Official Guide To Buying Final Expense Life Insurance

14 BEST BURIAL INSURANCE FOR SMOKERS

Since getting my life insurance license in 2011, I've met thousands of tobacco users. And many of these smokers worry about the price they will pay for their burial insurance.

However, while tobacco usage causes higher prices, working with the right agent minimizes the actual price you'll pay for your burial insurance. Who wants to pay more than necessary, right?

Tobacco Users - Avoid These Burial Insurance Products!

First things first. Make sure when getting a quote for burial insurance that you avoid "guaranteed acceptance life insurance," or "no-questions asked life insurance."

While premiums may seem competitive, the truth is those plans do not give first day full coverage. What does this mean? If you die within the first two years of the policy, your beneficiary does not receive the full death benefit.

Actually, the beneficiary only receives premiums paid back plus interest. That's horrible!

Look at it this way. If you die of natural causes twelve months into your guaranteed acceptance life insurance plan, your beneficiary may only receive several hundred dollars back. And this is not enough to properly pay for a burial.

What should you do? Make sure that you work with a broker. Brokers shop a variety of competitively-priced burial insurance companies. This gives you much better odds at both high-quality, full-coverage burial insurance, all at a competitive price.

What If I Smoke And Have COPD?

Sometimes, smokers have a COPD diagnosis. Moreover, they are concerned their diagnosis eliminates eligibility for quality insurance.

Here's the good news. When working with a broker, you can commonly find first-day full coverage. Even if you have a diagnosis of COPD, bronchitis, emphysema, or lung disease.

Unfortunately, many companies you see on TV and in the mail force you to wait two years before fully protecting you against natural causes of death. Increase your chances of avoiding this and work with a broker.

What If I Smoke Cigars?

Historically, cigar smokers have an easier time of qualifying for life insurance coverage than smokers. While not always the case, cigar smokers can qualify for preferred non-tobacco rates more often than not.

At Buy Life Insurance For Burial, we work with carriers that rate cigar usage at non-tobacco rates. In many circumstances, we have saved clients hundreds of dollars a year on their life insurance. How? Because we work with carriers that view cigar smokers as having less serious health consequences, compared to cigarette users.

Also, frequency of cigar smoking doesn't matter. More so, the cigar smoker can smoke daily, and he'll still qualify for non-smoker rates.

What If I Dip Or Chew Tobacco?

Perhaps it's because I live in the Southeast, but I commonly run into people who chew tobacco or dip snuff. And many worry they cannot afford higher premiums associated with tobacco usage.

Luckily, insurance carriers rate chewing and dipping like cigar usage. Both are considered non-smoker rates with several insurance companies.

How To Secure The Best Rates For Tobacco Users

First, make sure you're working with a broker. This gives you the most assurance you're getting the best price for your burial insurance as a tobacco user.

Second, pricing for burial insurance on smokers ranges wildly. I've seen pricing differences on burial insurance premiums of $40 to $50 a month. And these are for identical plans.

15 ABOUT THE AUTHOR

David Duford has been a licensed life insurance agent since 2011. David specializes in the final expense burial life insurance market, where he shops for the best combination of price and coverage for his clients interested in life insurance.

David also owns and operates a national life insurance agency called Final Expense Agent Mentor, where he teaches agents how to help people interested in buying quality final expense life insurance coverage.

David is also the author of The Official Guide To Selling Final Expense Insurance, has written for the Insurance Forum, and actively contributes video content for consumers and agents on his YouTube channel.

If you are interested in having David help you find a final expense life insurance policy, call 888-626-0439, visit www.BuyLifeInsuranceForBurial.com for more information, or email him at info@buylifeinsuranceforburial.com.

Made in the USA
Monee, IL
13 January 2025

76511867R00046